FOREWARD

There is nothing that delights the heart of a father more than seeing his sons and daughters discover and walk in their God given destiny. David Wagner is one of those sons who has brought great pleasure and blessing to my heart and tens of thousands of others around the world as we have had the privilege to be a part of this wonderful miracle.

You are about to read an incredible story of God's love, grace and mercy. You will never again wonder if God is interested in your future and destiny.

The Lord has certainly fulfilled His promise that David would go around the world and preach the Gospel seeing lives touched and changed. I have watched Dave walk through the past 15 years of life and ministry. I have been with him in those challenging places in life, and I have been with him when he has released powerful prophetic words, to kings, presidents, corporate

*executives, and political and religious
leaders. I have seen the miracles and
witnessed the great harvest of souls as
he has declared the Gospel of Jesus to
the multitudes around the world.*

*It has been a joy watching him grow to
be a strong leader in the Kingdom of
God as well as an amazing husband
and father. God has blessed him with
his beautiful wife Molly who has been a
strong and stabilizing force in his life.
His 5 wonderful children are a living
testimony of a man who leads his house
well. All of these things and more prove
that no matter what your past or
circumstance, you can still discover and
fulfill your divine purpose in life.*

*As a spiritual father, I am so proud of
who David has become and am excited
about what the future still holds.*

*May you be blessed as you read this
story of God's Amazing Grace in the life
of a young man who could have been a
statistic of this fatherless generation.*

Because he has discovered the blessing of Sonship in the Family of God, he is now releasing the Fathers Heart to his generation.

Lindell Ballenger

Senior Pastor

Jubilee International Ministries

Pensacola, Florida

DEDICATION

This book is dedicated to the memory of my Grandmother Johanna Ridderhoff. Her faith, love, and prayers have helped make me who I am. She always saw something in me that I could not see in myself. I love and miss her very much.

THANKS

Thank you Lord Jesus for sealing my adoption and giving your all for me.

I would like to thank my beautiful wife Molly for all of her love, support, and patience. Molly you truly are the best thing that ever happened to me outside of accepting Jesus. Thank you for selfless love and for giving me the greatest 5 kids on the planet

To my children: Arah, Benjamin, Caleb, Joshua, and Isaac. Thank you for sharing me with the world and for giving me lots of sermon stories.

Thank you Pastor B for writing the forward to this book and for your constant love, encouragement and insight.

To my church family at Jubilee for your continual love, support, and prayers.

Pastor Len for pushing me and challenging me to change and for being a friend that sticks closer than a brother.

A special thanks to Clint Gilliland who made this project a reality and who has been a constant friend and brother in arms.

I am eternally grateful to Earon James for giving deadlines that I never keep, to Craig Lawrence for creating the cover of the book, to Michelle Crawford and Michelle Mobley for their graceful editing and words of encouragement.

MOTORCYCLES FOR MISSIONS

Reaching farther ...

To date, we have given away over 30 Motorcycles to missionaries and pastors in Uganda, Mozambique, Nicaragua, Cambodia, Kenya, Burundi, Zambezia, Mozambique anda 3 wheeled Motorcycle in Ghana. We have also bought a 4X4 Toyota pickup truck for Pastor Bladimir and Ministerio Amigos de Dios to support them in feeding over 500 children in the garbage dumps of Managua every day.

How Can You Help?

You can cover the cost of one motorcycle and all the necessary equipment for $1500, or give a donation of any amout to go toward this powerful initiative.

To donate, simply go to fathersheartministries.org and click the donate button, or mail your donation to:

Fathers Heart Ministries
5910 North W Street Pensacola, FL 32505

two wheels at a time!

In the natural world, I would be a statistic, just another casualty of life. Like many in America and around the world today, I grew up without a father. I am the youngest of five children; when I was five years old my dad got diagnosed with a malignant brain tumor, and he passed away when I was six years old, His death came just one week before Christmas. This was one of the most life altering events in my life. Fortunately, my mother and grandmother with the help of three loving older sisters raised me.

My mom and grandma were women of faith, and they made me go to church. In fact, church was never an option in my life. As long as I lived under my mother's roof, I was in church Wednesday nights and twice on Sundays. I was not always happy about that, but today I am forever thankful. We often quote the scripture, Proverbs 22:6 that states, "Train up a child in the way that they should go, even when they are old they will not depart from it". This does not mean that they will not stray from the way, but it does mean that they will always find and be able to return to the way you have taught them.

Shortly after my father died, I was

playing in my room when I heard the voice of the Lord for the very first time. "Son, I have called you to go around the world preaching the Gospel. Everywhere you go lives are going to be touched and changed." Honestly because, I did not know any better. I put on a bathrobe because preachers wore robes back then. I made a fake microphone, lined up my stuffed animals on my bed, and started preaching. I think Teddy was about to get saved; G.I. Joe was about to get healed and Care Bear was about to get delivered when my mom and grandma walked in the room. I will never forget the look of surprise on their face and the question: David, What are you doing?"

"The Lord spoke to me..." I replied; "He told me, I will be going to go around the world preaching the gospel and wherever I go lives are going to be touched and changed." Now the two most important people in my life looked surprised and worried at the same time. "Who spoke to you?" My mom asked. Again I responded; "The Lord spoke to me."

This was not necessarily a common or familiar experience in the conservative mainline church I was raised in. Before, I tell you what happened next, I want you to know that I am thankful for my heritage, and I believe my mother and grandmother did the right thing, when they had brought me to see the Pastor. As we walked into the office and sat down, my mom said, "Please tell the pastor what you told us."

So I did. "Pastor the Lord spoke to me; He said, "Son I've called you to go around the world preaching the Gospel. Wherever you go lives are going to be touched and changed."

I was not prepared for his response. He grew more irritated with every word I spoke. His face turned red then purple as he picked up his giant print King James Bible and continued to shake it at me. "Boy, get it through your head, God does not speak today. He does not heal today. Those things may have happened 2,000 years ago, but they do not happen today." He then told my mother; "If I were you, I would take him to see a psychiatrist. He must be having a hard time dealing with the death of his father." Again, I want you to know that I believe my mother did the right thing. She listened to the counsel of her pastor. However, the outcome of *this meeting would altar and change my relationship with God, as I knew him for many years to come.*

"I think your son is struggling with the loss of his father and has severe depression and I am concerned that he is having these "hallucinations" because of your family history. Your son may be a schizophrenic. We need to put him on some medications and start him in counseling right away."

Mental illness was no stranger to my family. There have been numerous suicides and "nervous breakdowns" throughout my family tree.

If you hear something spoken over you enough times I believe that eventually you will start believing it. If you start believing it, you will start receiving it. Then Unfortunately, you will start manifesting it.

There is no doubt in my mind today, that once God announced my prophetic destiny that the enemy came immediately to steal the word. God is not a respecter of persons and neither is the enemy. The devil will even use well-meaning, church going Christians to try to thwart your destiny. Therefore, it is crucial that you know what God has said about you and you must also know who you are in Christ.

It did not take long for me to make up my mind about everything that was happening to me and being said to me. First, I came to some very fast conclusions about God. At the age of seven, I figured that if God could not speak, could not heal, and obviously He did not raise my father from the dead, then simply God was not real. If He is real, He could not be good and did not care. Shortly after this realization, I smoked my first cigarette at the age of nine. I started drinking, by twelve. I was becoming a miserable soul on the inside. I encountered some of the most traumatic experiences of my life from 7-13 years of age, as well. I was sexually molested by three different people including being sodomized with a beer bottle. I had very little self worth and lived most days severely depressed or even worse numb. Numb is an extremely dangerous condition to be in because if you do not "feel", it as if you are already dead.

By the time I was 13 I was severely suicidal. I remember

thinking, nothing is ever going to change. I am better off dead. I began hearing voices in my head: "Go ahead, kill yourself! You're worthless!" One afternoon I mustered up the "courage" to hang myself with a rope from the rafters in my family's' garage. I carefully tied the rope, stood on the ladder, took a deep breath and jumped off. Somehow miraculously the rope broke. I was on an emotional roller coaster trying to figure out who I was. Often, I found myself riding my bicycle to the cemetery and sitting on my father's grave. Usually I would bring a six pack of my father's favorite beer and a pack of his favorite cigarettes. "One for you, and one for me." It was how I tried to identify with him. I would try to talk to my dad. I used to cry and scream, "Why did you leave me? What did I do? Why don't you love me?" I needed identity and was on a quest for significance.

The despair continued into my high school years. Although, I had grown up in the public school system, my mom wanted me to go to a Christian High School. In this school, if somebody wanted a laugh, I would provide it. My personal goal was to be as disruptive, funny, and tormenting as possible. I did manage to set a school record in my four years. I hold the record for detentions and in-school suspensions for a semester. Most teachers and people tolerated who I was, but a small delegation of teachers and friends celebrated me. Through the love of a few, I found a voice in me that I didn't know was there. Looking back, I can now see how God used them to give me glimpses of hope. In my senior year, I felt like I was done with living. I wanted to die and did not see an alternative way out. I fired up my 1977 Monte Carlo and attempted to drive it into Lake Michigan in downtown, Chicago. As I put the car in drive and pushed the accelerator to the floor, and began to pick up momentum when the unthinkable happened. My car ran out of gas. To my surprise somehow (God) I had a hole in my gas tank. Talk about frustration. A few months later, on the anniversary of my father's death, I decided to leave school and drive as fast as I could into a canal across the street. There was just one problem. I hit a semi-truck. The car was wrecked, but I survived without a bump, bruise, or scratch. I had my seatbelt properly fastened. Hey, I wanted to die... I did not want to get hurt.

I graduated high school with a 1.97 grade point average and got accepted into a Christian College. In my first semester, I started working with campus security for a little extra cash and to meet female students. While working Halloween night, a Police Sergeant came through the campus parking lot and started talking to me. We really kind of hit it off, and he told me about a cadet program that could help me launch a career in law enforcement. I

*jumped at the opportunity,
because eight of my father's
brothers were Chicago Police
Officers. Maybe this would finally
help me know who I was. I had
great success for the first four
years, until I could not show up for
duty on time. Normally I was to
drunk the night before and slept
through my alarm clocks. I also
pushed the boundaries of authority
and violated general orders not to
mention two involuntary trips to
the local mental ward because of
threats of suicide. I became a
liability and was graciously given
the choice of resigning or being
fired. My relationships were all*

falling a part. I was a failure and isolated myself. I tried shooting myself with a .38 caliber handgun. I pulled the trigger of the fully loaded gun. The hammer hit the bullet, but the bullet did not come out of the gun. When that weapon failed, I loaded my 9 mm. Again I pulled the trigger; the hammer hit the bullet but the bullet did not come out of the gun. You know that you are pretty messed up when you can't even kill yourself right!

On Easter Sunday 1994, I was drunk as a skunk. Now, I have never seen a drunk skunk, but I am sure it smells bad and looks pretty funny. When I stumbled into my apartment, I pressed the play button on my answering machine. "If you want to see Gram while she is still alive, you need to get to Rest Haven as fast as possible. She had a massive stroke and is in a coma." I found someone to give me a ride and went to see the most influential person in my life. As I walked into the room, I could hear the sound of the "death rattle" as her lungs were being filled with fluid. It was an awkward setting as I walked in to find my mom, step-dad, a pastor and other family who I had not seen in months. We were all saying good-byes to the woman who had changed and formed most of our lives. Within a few moments, the unthinkable happened and my little grandma scared the snot out of all of us in the room. She sat straight up the bed and began to sing.... "My Jesus I love thee, I know thou art mine. To thee all the folly of sin I resign..." She would lie back down and slip back into a coma. She managed to sit up four more times and finish the song. We said our good-byes around 2AM. I was haunted by what I had witnessed and remember and thinking to myself, "You wouldn't sing praises to God that close to death unless

He was real." The next day I woke up and returned to Rest Haven to see if my grandma made it through the night. When I walked into her room, I was surprised to find her not only alive but sitting up in her bed eating Rusk (a hard biscuit from Holland) and drinking hot tea from a saucer. As I stepped across the threshold of her room, she looked up. I saw something I had never experienced before. My grandmother looked angry. Then I found out why. She said; "David I know that you were here last night. It was my night to go home and be with the Lord, but He kept me alive to tell you this... "I am sorry we did not believe you when you told us the Lord spoke to you when you were six. We just did not understand. God has not changed His mind about you. He has called you to go around the world preaching the Gospel. Everywhere you go lives are going to be touched and changed." Then she told me the words I could not believe. "... And you will be the one to win your brother." Fifteen minutes after my grandmother gave me that word she went home to be with Lord.

For the next three years, I would

continue running from the Lord. I found myself diving into addiction and insanity. I tried to find love in numerous immoral relationships and found myself falling deeper into realms of darkness. One night while I was at a party with some old friends, somebody brought out an Ouija board. I thought such things like this were stupid and make believe. To prove how dumb it was I grabbed the "spinner" and started asking questions. To my dismay and unbelief, this demonic tool beneath my fingers began to move and spin. I did not know what was happening, but I did know that something was making this thing move. In our drunken stupidity we began to call for dead people to come and speak to us. Before we knew it, we were in over our heads and opened doors to demonic realms. I can pin point this night, because it was the night when my problems went to a whole new level.

Running from God is never very smart, and that is even truer if you have a word from the Lord hanging over your life. In the midst of all the torment, all the shame, and chaos of my life, there was no escaping my grandma's final words to me. Nonetheless, I slipped further and further into the miserable cycle of chemical dependence and codependent living. I wanted to be loved, and I desired to love, but truthfully I did not know how to do either. How do you receive what you do not feel worthy of, and how do you give what you do not have?

In July of 1994, I knew I had to make a change. I lost my job, my place to live, and what little pride I had left. It was time to move where nobody knew me so that I could be whoever I wanted to be. Thanks to some college friends, I moved to Wisconsin. Finally, I

*thought things could be different.
There was just one big problem... I
had a different address but the
same demons. I tried to fake it
until I could make it, but eventually
the same cycles of addiction,
manipulation, and insanity would
manifest themselves.*

*I met a young woman and fell in
love. We did all the things that you
shouldn't do before you get
married. We were on a quick path
to personal destruction. There was
one major problem in our
relationship. That problem was
that she had a praying mother.
This woman was bold enough to*

believe the whole Bible. Every time I saw her, she would tell me she loved and that she was praying for me. I remember thinking "You do not know me, so you cannot love me...and keep your prayers to yourself." After a few months of dating, we moved in together. This decision pushed my relationship with my mom and stepdad even more distant and turbulent. We were married in August of 1995, but things were never very happy. To my surprise my wife decided to give her life back to the Lord. In Christian terms, she got saved. I honestly thought that this would be a passing fad. I continued to fall deeper and deeper into depression, addiction, and by now the symptoms of schizophrenia were beginning to really manifest themselves. To make matters worse, I was being rejected in the worse possible way. I would be drinking in a bar or with my "buddies" and an unusual phenomenon would begin to occur. I like to call this phenomenon "P.W.I." (Preaching While Intoxicated). I do not know how or why (other than God has an amazing sense of humor) but I would be sitting there and all of a sudden look at the guy next to me *or even to the bartender and say stuff like, "Jesus loves you man. He died on the cross for your sins man." And then I would start bawling like a baby. Usually this would lead to the walk of shame after getting kicked out of the bar. One time a bartender told me, "Dude, make up your mind. Be a preacher or be a drinker, but you can't be both. Even I know that!" It is pretty bad when misery does not want company. Just when I thought things could not get any worse, my wife gave me an ultimatum. "If you want to stay with me, you have to go to church." Well, I do not like ultimatums but I don't like sleeping out in the cold either. Besides, I really thought this church thing was not going to last, and that eventually, I could win her back to the "dark side".*

When that dreadful day came, I gave an ultimatum of my own. "I will go to church with you. If anything crazy happens, I am out of there. If anybody rolls in the aisles, like you holy rollers do, I am out of there. If anyone speaks in them tongues, I am out of there." Well, it did not take very long for "it" to happen. On the particular Sunday I came to church, there was a guest preacher. This guy was a missionary to Spain, and he honestly looked like a clown. He was wearing red pants, rainbow suspenders, big clown shoes and he even had a flower that sprayed water. To make matters worse, he preached while riding a unicycle and juggling fruit. "Let's get out of here! This guy is crazy!" After receiving a few elbows to the side, I finally quired down and decided that I would struggle my way through all the craziness. At one point the preacher paused and then "it" happened. A little old lady three rows in front of me shouted out in tongues. I tried to get up

and run out of the church, but I
could not move. It was as if my
butt was glued to the seat. I
listened in awe and disbelief as
the preacher gave the
interpretation. "There is a young
man here today. You are twenty
six years old and have been
running from God all of your life.
God spoke to you when you were
six years old and again a few
years ago through your
grandmother on her deathbed.
The world has called you
worthless, but I call you valuable.
The world has called you
schizophrenic and alcoholic, but I
call you son. Son I have not

changed my mind about you. I have called you to go around the world preaching the gospel. Everywhere you go lives are going to be touched and changed, and you will be the one to win your brother." I wept like a baby, but I did not respond. I was in shock, and I was angry. Who told this guy these things? I have never told anyone about these things. Somebody is trying to set me up, I thought.

From this point on, my world unraveled even more. I started hearing voices more frequently. I would often find myself hours

*away from home not knowing
where I was or how I got there. I
was hospitalized and
institutionalized on a regular basis.
All of this was more than my wife
could handle and she filed for
divorce while I was in a "halfway"
house." This was just another blow
that stirred up every rejection and
abandonment issue in my soul. I
tried to get her to reconcile, but
nothing I tried to manipulate
worked. I went to her parents. I
went to her church. I faked faith
and started going to church to win
her back, but it was over. A few
days before the divorce was final, I
went to a bar and built up what I*

used to call "liquid courage". I was going to win her back and that was that. I drove to her house, knocked on the door, and tried to persuade her that I could change. She was not buying what I was selling and decided to she head for her car to leave. I followed her and fought the voices that were screaming at me to. "Run her off the road. If you can't have her, nobody should have her. Kill her and yourself." She pulled over on the side of the road, and I pulled in behind her. However, I didn't see the police car in front of her. Now I was not just going to get divorced, I was going to jail. This was my second drunk driving offense in a matter of six months.

On January 17th, 1997, I thought my life was over. I finished working a night shift at a factory, went to the bar for a couple shots, and went home to get cleaned up for my court date. It was over in a matter of minutes. The room was filled with couples there to dissolve their marriages. The judge went through the motions and technicalities and we signed some paperwork, and I chalked up another failure in life. I had nothing left to live for and nothing left to lose. There was only one way out, and that one way out was suicide. I drank a bottle of gin and a twelve pack of beer and took over two hundred and fifty prescription pills, and I laid down to die or so I thought. Somehow I ended up in church twelve miles away from where I was living in front of a Pastor who just happened to be starting his first day on the job. Now the Lord has a sense of humor for sure, because this happened to be a church from the same denomination I grew up in. I proceeded to drop dead in this poor man's office. He did not know what was happening, and he did not believe in resurrection, so he called 911. The fire station was less than a block away, so I was down only for a short time. The paramedics revived me and brought me to the hospital where they pumped my stomach. I spent two days in a coma.

At this point, in my life, I being estranged from my family, nobody knew where I was at or what had happened. Somehow the hospital managed to track down my mom. "Mrs. Hoekstra? We have your son, David in ICU. It does not look good, and we do not expect him to live. In all honesty, if he does live he will most likely be a vegetable

*and need to be institutionalized
the rest of his life."*

*My mother did what she has done
all of her life. She prayed. "Lord
you gave him to me, and now I
give him to you. I named him
David because I always wanted
him to be a shepherd like David in
the Bible."*

*After two days in a coma, a bright
light came in the room, and I
heard the Lord speak to me for the
fourth time in my life. He said,
"Son, I have not changed my mind
about you. I have called you to go
around the world preaching the*

Gospel. Wherever you go, lives are going to be touched and changed. Today, I set before you the choice between life and death. If you chose me, I will save you, heal you, deliver you, and you will fulfill your destiny. If not, then this is where you will go..." The Lord then took me by the hand and led me to what I can only describe as the outer banks of hell. I could smell the sulfur and hear the screams coming from what seemed like never ending darkness. I heard the cries of acquaintances, friends, and family members that had died without the Lord. They were screaming at me.

"Why didn't you tell me this place was real? You went to church all of your life. Why didn't you tell us?" When I came to, I actually felt something I had never felt before. I felt unconditional love and overwhelming peace. My first prayer was, "God, if you can love me, when I cannot love myself, I will serve you the rest of the days of my life."

Over the course of the next three to four months, everything began to change. Jesus had started the process of transformation. I was a work in progress, and everyday seemed to get brighter. There were numerous hoops to jump through. I completed various medical and legal processes to prove my new found sanity. I had literally been labeled as an incorrigible of society. Simply put, in the eyes of the states of Illinois and Wisconsin, I had no value, potential, and no future.

God worked many miracles on my behalf. On Good Friday, 1997, I was officially removed from state, medical care, and all medications.

Freedom is a process. Freedom also is a choice. When you have been bound and captive most of your life, you have to learn how to live free. In essence, I knew how to live bound and I knew how to be "crazy", but freedom was brand new to me. I quickly realized the need to grow in my new found faith, and I also had an insatiable desire to belong to something bigger than me. I went to an average of three churches every Sunday trying to figure out where I fit. One Sunday night, I was sitting in my apartment flipping through the channels, when a preacher named John Osteen from Texas grabbed my attention. He was preaching on the baptism of the Holy Spirit and repeatedly shouted, "How big is your want to?" I was convinced that there was more than what I knew, and there was a whole lot more than what I experienced! I have to admit, I was a little naive and found myself going to a Baptist church on a Wednesday night seeking after the "Baptism of the Holy Spirit." I was politely sent down the road to explore other churches in my pursuit. I visited dozens of churches, searching for more! I found myself going to a noon hour prayer meeting everyday for a month asking, seeking, knocking, and even begging God for the Baptism of the Spirit. One day I was so tired *of going through the motions and trying to get man to help me and explain things to me, I decided to get really, really, bold! I left the prayer meeting, and while driving down the road, I cried out to the Lord. "Lord, I want all that you have for me! If it's real, I want it! I read in your Word about tongues and I want it!" And then He did it! He filled me up while I was driving 70 miles per hour down Interstate 43. It was just He and I. There were no more excuses, no more doubts, just the results of seeking Him. Everyday was an adventure in God, and I couldn't wait for what He would do or say next.*

December 27, 1997 while I was at an all night men's prayer meeting, I was lying face down crying out to the Lord and found myself with an appointment with destiny. I kept hearing, "Move to Pensacola. Move to Pensacola." I never heard of Pensacola before, but the voice of the Lord was loud and clear. I spoke to the Pastor in the morning he said, "I don't know why He would tell you to go there, but I know of five people that will be very happy, because they need a ride to Bible college in Pensacola for the spring semester. Two weeks later, I loaded up my 1989

Ford Aerostar that did not have reverse and left Wisconsin with $141 in my pocket and headed to Pensacola - a place I had never heard of and a place I had never been. Half way through the trip, somewhere in the middle of Tennessee, I began to have second thoughts. "Where am I going? What am I going to do when I get there?" As I inquired of the Lord and asked these questions, He simply spoke: "I am taking you to a place called there!"

When I arrived in Pensacola, I got the students dropped off at Bible College and thought I would apply.

Maybe this is the reason why I am here. They quickly rejected me and today I am extremely thankful for that decision. I did not really know where I was or where I was going. I found myself driving around a new city asking the obvious question, "What am I doing here?" After driving aimlessly, I pulled into a subdivision called, "Montage". I pulled into a driveway and opened my door to push myself backwards. As I said earlier, my van did not have reverse. When suddenly a man and woman came out of the garage and asked me a jaw dropping question,

"Are you David Wagner?"

You could imagine my surprise.

"Yes, how did you know?" I replied.

"We were in Wisconsin on a business trip and wandered into a Christian book store. The store manager, David heard us talking and asked us if we were from the area. When we told him we were from Pensacola, he was extremely excited and told us your story. We gave him our contact information. Did he talk to you?"

I did not know what to say. I knew David from a church I had been attending but I had not seen or talked to him since my departure from Wisconsin. I did not have a cell phone or pager back then, so for me to turn up in Dan and Carolyn's driveway was nothing less than supernatural. The Weaver's invited me to stay with them for a few nights. After the first night, they asked me if I would like to stay with them while I got settled in Pensacola. What an answer to prayer and comfort to know that I was wanted.

That first month in Pensacola was exciting and frustrating all at the same time. First of all, I felt like the Lord played a trick on me. Pensacola did not look like the Florida I imagined. In fact, it seemed more like L.A. (Lower Alabama) than Florida. I was hungry for destiny and longed to find the place that I could fit. I was hungry for God and just wanted Him. I would go to everything that seemed spiritual. If a church had a sign that said "Revival", I was there. I must have attended over twenty church services that first month in Pensacola, but I didn't feel at home anywhere I went. Finally, frustration was wearing me down.

On Saturday night February 14th, 1998 I gave God an ultimatum. Go ahead and laugh. God did. I shook my fist at heaven and screamed,

"Why am I here? God if you don't show me where I belong, I am out of here!"

I heard the Lord then respond and say," Where would you go? What do you have to go back too? This is your year for Jubilee."

I was furious. I had read all the church signs and saw the word Jubilee all over Christian television. I screamed, "I know it's the year of Jubilee but I do not even know what that means!" The Lord then made it plain: "Open the phone book." There was the ad that changed my life, forever. Jubilee International Ministries. I showed up the next morning with expectation. I put on my one and only suit. It was pea soup green and to this day my Pastor doesn't let me forget about that suit. When I walked through the glass doors, I was met with open arms by two of the most amazing people I have ever met. Harold and Barbara Bowling welcomed me. I will never forget my first encounter with Harold. "What is your name son?" He asked. "David Wagner" I replied.

He looked me straight in the eyes and said, "Come on in son. You are a mighty man of God."

I wondered, "What did he say, and what does that mean?"

I like to say I survived my first Jubilee service. It was unlike anything I have ever seen or experienced. It was loud, it was long, and it was intense. Pastor Ballenger not only preached with passion, he stood on the chairs. "Could you do this in church?" I wondered. I left at the altar call and stared at the welcome packet. I kept reading it over and over. I went home and laid down on my bed. "Go back to the service tonight." I heard the Lord say. "No way I thought." As I processed what I had seen and heard. The next day while I was working the Lord spoke again, "Go to the prayer meeting at Jubilee." As much as I hate to admit it, I did not go. In fact I went to see the movie "Titanic" instead.

Tuesday morning, the Lord spoke again, "Go to the prayer meeting tonight." I found myself going to the mall instead. As I parked my van, the Lord shook me and asked, "Where did I tell you to go?"

"The prayer meeting," I responded fearfully. "Where did you go last night" the Lord asked?

"Lord, you know," I quickly responded.

"Tell me!" asked the Lord. "To see

the Titanic," I said shamefully.
I will never forget what He said
next, "If you do not get to that
prayer meeting, you will have a
Titanic experience."

As I walked into the auditorium,
people were pacing, shouting,
speaking in English, Spanish, and
tongues. It was intense and
honestly quite uncomfortable. I
think it ended about 8 o'clock, and
I survived. As I walked up the
center aisle to leave. I felt a hand
grab my hand. It was the hand of
Pastor Len. "What's your name
buddy?" he asked.
"David," I responded.

Then he spoke the words I will never forget. "Do you know that you have a call of God on your life? God has called you to do something incredible. You are going to go around the world and preach the gospel." I stood there shocked and weeping. I had finally found the place called "there". I am proud to say Pastor Len Ballenger became my friend, my mentor, and my Pastor. He saw something in me that I could not see in myself. I was inducted into an elite group affectionately known as L cubed. "Len's Lovable Losers." Within a few months, I was hooked. I was fully immersed

*into life at the "Jube" as we call it. I
fell deeper in love with God and
just wanted to serve him. A few
months later, I found myself
meeting Pastor B and a group
from the church over to Bay
Minnette, Alabama where Pastor
was preaching at a conference. I
was wearing the infamous pea
green soup smoking a cigarette
when the church van pulled up to
the parking lot. I quickly put out
the smoke and hoped nobody saw
me. Smoking was the only
addiction I did not get delivered
from at my salvation.*

*I sat in the back of the church
away from anyone else. I was*

changing but still terribly uncomfortable around people especially if I thought they might reject me. As Pastor "continued" to close his message and start the altar call, I got up to leave. To my surprise, he called me out. "Son come down here a minute. God has been dealing with me about you. Come here and pray for this young man." It was my first time and I cannot even begin to describe what I felt flow through my veins. Pastor Ballenger would tell me later how he argued with the Lord. He did not really know me. Should he trust me since I was seen smoking a few hours earlier? I will never forget that night. It was the first time I ever prophesied, and it was the first time I ever saw a miracle through my own hands. I was overwhelmed, undone, and in absolute awe as Jesus healed and created new kidneys in this young man I prayed for.

From this moment on I was consumed with whatever I could do to serve in the local church. I became an usher, greeter, catcher, janitor, and all around servant. However, it was more than servanthood to me. I did not just want to be a servant, I wanted to live as a son in the House of God. The message of sonship is and continues to be a message that consumes me and provokes me to build Him a house where He can live. In those early days of ministry my host family moved away from Pensacola. I was given the opportunity to stay with Pastor Ballenger and Pastor Darlene for a few weeks. I came for two weeks and I stayed for almost two years. These were formative days in my life and early walk with the Lord. A common saying in our church culture is: "More is caught in the kingdom than taught in the kingdom." I found myself with the great honor of being hired to work full time with the church and our Christian Academy. I was the cook and the janitor and loved every waking minute. I made about $128 per week but this was better than a million dollars to me. I worked most days from 6:30 AM to 11:00PM and would not trade one moment for anything this world has to offer. Over and over God would meet me in unusual places and at unusual times.

One Monday night after a prayer meeting, I was cleaning the ladies restroom. I was the only one in the building and enjoying some alone

*time with the Lord. When all of a
sudden I got the revelation that
this was not just a job or
expression of servanthood but
rather this is what Paul might have
been trying to express when he
wrote Romans 12:1 "Therefore, I
urge you, brothers, in view of
God's mercy, to offer your bodies
as living sacrifices, holy and
pleasing to God," this is your
spiritual act of worship.*

*As I worshipped the Lord, while
cleaning the toilet, God showed
up. A physical cloud filled the
room and I was undone. Pastor B
returned to the church and heard*

*noise from down the hall. He
followed the sound to the ladies
restroom. When he pushed the
door open, a cloud and a wind
pushed him backwards. This was
a divine encounter with the glory
of God.*

*I don't know where you began
your walk with the Lord or where
you were when He called you, but
He found me in a place of
surrender and humility hovering
over a toilet. I have often longed to
go back to the place He found me.
There was something so sweet
and powerful about those days.
That is why I continue to serve
whenever I am home. These were*

defining moments for my ministry.
In June 1998 Pastor Len took me
on my first ministry trip. We went
to Thief River Falls, Minnesota.
This is where I really began to give
the word of the Lord. After a
weeklong youth camp, we
ventured to Northern Manitoba,
Canada where I had my first
preaching opportunity. I managed
to mumble for seven minutes while
drawing circles with my toe on the
platform. I turned the service back
over to Len and I am sure he must
have thought he missed God and
wondered if I was ever called to
preach. He rescued me and kept
pushing me to practice my gifts.

The next night I was primed and ready. The prophetic and power of God exploded out of me. I had tapped into something bigger than I could ever dream or imagine - something called Divine Destiny.

In the beginning days of my walk with God, I had more zeal than brains. One night during one of our prophetic gatherings a friend gave me a word that I would raise the dead. I had a child like faith that believed that if God said it I could do it - now not later. Later that week I found myself practicing. I would dress up and go to visitations and funerals of

*people I didn't know. As I walked
past the casket, I would simply
touch the dead body and whisper,
"In the name of Jesus rise."
I also had a friend who was in
charge of cleaning at a local
hospital. He showed me where the
morgue was, and I would sneak in
and "practice" until I got caught
and banned from one local
hospital. I may have not had much
wisdom, but I had faith that Jesus
would raise the dead, and I was
determined to see it in my life and
ministry. I still pray for the dead to
come to life. I figure the worse
thing that can happen is that they
stay dead. I was simply rehearsing*

for what I have now seen manifest in my life and ministry.

I met my wife Molly in January 1999. Her mom was a volunteer at the school and had encouraged me to meet her daughter and granddaughter. I thought to myself, "If she is your daughter she is probably too young, and I am not interested in a "built-in family." My mother-in-law is one of the most persistent women I know. She kept inviting me to every event, get together, and even Thanksgiving dinner. I would never show up, but my curiosity was getting the best of me. I finally

*showed up on January 9, 1999. I
think I fell immediately in love.
After Molly played hard to get for a
week, we started our journey
together. We got engaged the
night before Mother's Day and
were well on our way towards
preparing for marriage, family, and
ministry. We had gotten saved and
filled with the Holy Spirit around
the same time. We were on the
fast track, or so we thought. We
were both working at the Christian
School, and I was somewhat of a
prophetic prodigy.
I would prophesy to everything
that moved.*

Molly and I were passionate about everything - maybe too passionate. We had a strong calling, but weak character and we put ourselves into compromising positions and fell into sexual sin. Molly became pregnant, and we went into denial. We hid the pregnancy for over four months, but we knew that we could not hide this forever. We were afraid to say the least. What would happen? We were certainly going to lose our jobs. I'm sure Pastor was going to kick me out of his house. What would people think? I finally worked up the courage to at least tell Pastor Len, his son.

He is like a brother to me and one of my dearest friends. I remember weeping in his office together and sensing the love he showed me. I also remember the words he spoke, "You have to tell Dad." I quickly blurted out, "No, that's why I told you." He basically gave me until the rest of the day to come clean.

However, I was afraid and full of shame. I went back into run and hide mode. I worked that day at the church in total shock and paranoia. Every time I saw Pastor B coming, I ran the other way and hid. I raced home that night hoping to get in the house, up the stairs, and into bed before Pastor could get home. Just in case, I packed my bags and waited for the worst. I laid in the bed. My chest was pounding, and all that I could think of was what a failure I was. It didn't take very long, and I heard the garage door open followed by deliberate footsteps up the stairs. It was the first time I ever heard the footsteps of a father. Pastor knocked on the door and said, "Dave, is there anything you need to talk to me about?"

I quickly responded; "No, sir." He insisted that I get up and meet him downstairs. Fear gripped me and I was sure that this was the beginning of the end of my short-lived ministry. As I sat down to talk to Pastor, I braced for the worst as I told him the whole truth. "I messed up and Molly is pregnant." The tears flowed down my face, and I was confident I was going to be kicked to the curb. However, the mercy of God and the love of a spiritual father filled the room. "Son, I am disappointed, but this does not change the call of God on your life.

There are consequences, but there is also restoration. Do you love Molly?"

I responded the obvious; "Yes." He said, "Well, let's make things *right and move up your wedding day."*

On December 11, 1999 I married the love of my life and best friend. The day was filled with love, support, and restoration from our church, family, and friends. While I was getting ready in a back room of the church, Harold Bowling came in to encourage me. He hugged my neck and asked, "Are you ready for this son?" I asked him if he could give me one word to sustain my marriage for eternity. His response was, "Commitment will sustain your marriage and your love. Commit to God and each other and everything else will fall in place." This may seem like a simple truth, but it has kept us through good times and bad. During our wedding, I addressed the congregation and confessed, "Today I am marrying my best friend. She is God's best for my life. I want you to hear it from me. We fell into sin and Molly is pregnant with my son. I am not marrying her because she is pregnant; I am marrying her because I love her. My son is not an accident and not a problem. He is a purpose and promise from God." Something happened that day that changed everything. I realized when you tell on yourself *the gossip stops, the judgment ends, accusations fall to the ground, and the devil has nothing else to say!*

Restoration took place over the following weeks and months. The process was not always easy. In fact, we tried to run away for a while. However, when true spiritual fathers and mothers surround you, they will refuse to let you go. That is why I am in ministry today. I have learned that the secret of success in life and in ministry is not in becoming something, but it is in being a son and walking in that identity and revelation. Molly and I were ordained into ministry in October 2001 and established Father's Heart Ministries shortly after. Over the past ten years we have had the honor to minister in thirty-five nations on six continents seeing thousands of lives saved, healed, transformed, and changed through the power of the Gospel. The only reason that any of this can even be possible is that before the foundations of the earth, He called me son. While I was a sinner, He called me son. While I was a failure, He called me son. When I wanted to quit, He called me son. Whenever I have succeeded, it is *because He called me son!*